Who Solves Issues?

Monika Davies

Consultant

Brian Allman
Principal
Upshur County Schools, West Virginia

Publishing Credits

Rachelle Cracchiolo, M.S.Ed., *Publisher*
Emily R. Smith, M.A.Ed., *SVP of Content Development*
Véronique Bos, *VP of Creative*
Dona Herweck Rice, *Senior Content Manager*
Dani Neiley, *Editor*
Fabiola Sepulveda, *Series Graphic Designer*

Image Credits: p8 Library of Congress [LC-DIG-hec-14201]; p9 Getty Images/Sarah Silbiger; p12 (top) City Clerk, City of New York; p13 (top) © Look and Learn/Bridgeman Images; p13 (bottom) Library of Congress [50050580]; p15 (bottom) Shutterstock/ Robert V Schwemmer; p16 (middle) Getty Images/The Washington Post; p20 (bottom) State of Alabama; p26 Getty Images/Hannah Peters; all other images from iStock and/or Shutterstock

Library of Congress Cataloging-in-Publication Data

Names: Davies, Monika, author.
Title: Who solves issues? / Monika Davies.
Description: Huntington Beach, CA : Teacher Created Materials, 2023. |
    Includes index. | Audience: Grades 4-6 | Summary: "Americans have issues
    they deal with every day. One person might worry about topsy-turvy
    potholes on their local roads. Another might want to challenge their
    country's economic policies. Issues can be local concerns. Others are
    national matters. So, who is in charge of helping citizens with these
    issues? The quick answer is the U.S. government. But there are different
    levels of government. Let's look at who solves what in America"--
    Provided by publisher.
Identifiers: LCCN 2022021303 (print) | LCCN 2022021304 (ebook) | ISBN
    9781087691121 (paperback) | ISBN 9781087691282 (ebook)
Subjects: LCSH: United States--Politics and government--Juvenile
    literature. | Federal government--United States--Juvenile literature. |
    State governments--United States--Juvenile literature. | Local
    government--United States--Juvenile literature.
Classification: LCC JK40 .D38 2023 (print) | LCC JK40 (ebook) | DDC
    320.973--dc23/eng/20220630
LC record available at https://lccn.loc.gov/2022021303
LC ebook record available at https://lccn.loc.gov/20220213048

5482 Argosy Avenue
Huntington Beach, CA 92649
www.tcmpub.com

ISBN 978-1-0876-9112-1
© 2023 Teacher Created Materials, Inc.

Table of Contents

Iowa State Capitol

Who Solves What?

All citizens have issues they care about. Issues are important topics that make a difference in people's lives. They come in all shapes and sizes. One citizen might worry about the potholes in their local roads. Another might want to challenge their country's economic policies. In 2020, the world faced a major public health issue: a global **pandemic**.

Americans have issues they deal with every day. Some are local concerns. Others are national matters. So, who is in charge of helping them with these issues? The quick answer is the U.S. government. The government was built to serve its people. It is tasked with trying to solve key issues in the country.

There are three levels of government in the United States. Each responds to different types of issues. The highest level is the federal government. It makes national decisions. These decisions have outcomes that affect all Americans. State governments are the second level. Their authority is also large. Lastly, there are local governments. The average person is most likely to **interact** with this level of government.

Every person has civic duties. One is to raise their voice when they have concerns. Speaking up is most effective when we talk to the right people. They are the ones who can help make change happen. This starts with knowing who solves what in America.

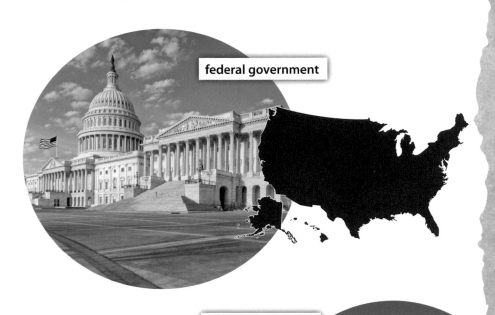

federal government

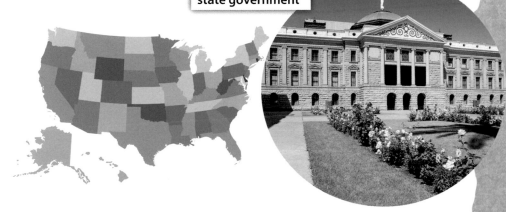

state government

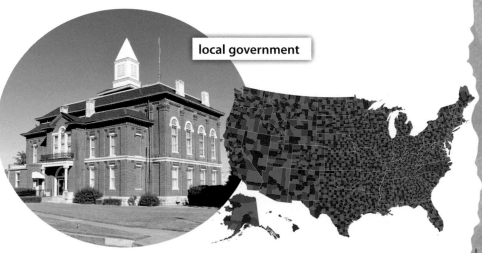

local government

Federal Focus

The federal government is the highest level of government in the United States. Some people call the federal level the "ultimate authority."

From a distance, it may seem like the federal level holds a lot of power. After all, they are at the top! Federal decisions affect all U.S. residents and citizens. These rulings can have a big impact on everyday lives. But the federal level has power in limited areas. All levels of government have this in common.

Federalism First

The United States is known for its federal system. **Federalism** is a type of government. This kind of system has at least two levels of government. Each level deals with certain issues. Responsibilities are split between the levels. This leads to a division of powers.

White House

This division of powers is crucial. It provides checks and balances. No level of government holds all the power. This ensures that one branch cannot simply "take over."

A federal system is **diverse**. It is also **unified**. In the United States, the federal level has national powers. This allows for unity. Decisions can be made with the whole country's interests in mind. But each state also has its own set of powers. This gives space for diverse **governance**. States across the country vary in their leadership.

Supreme Law

The people who wrote the U.S. Constitution were tasked to create unity—and much more. This document is a key part of the United States. It defines the "supreme law of the land." The Constitution sets up the federal government, fundamental laws, and basic rights for all Americans.

Federal Duties

So, what falls on the federal level's list of duties? For one, it is the only level of government that can **amend** the U.S. Constitution. Since 1789, many leaders have proposed amendments. Over 11,000 have been put forward. In total, only 27 amendments have been put into action. The last time it happened was 1992. It is no small act to change the Constitution!

The federal level can also declare war. It decides if the country will enter global **disputes**. It also maintains the U.S. military.

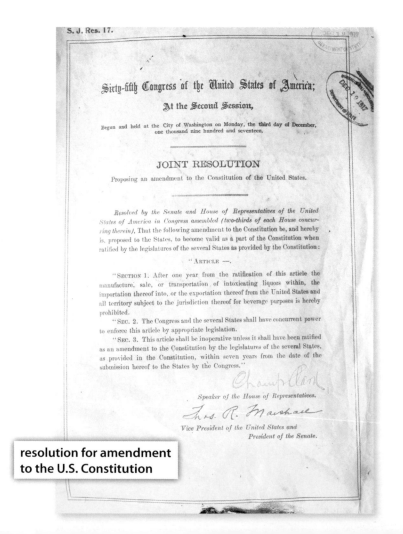

resolution for amendment
to the U.S. Constitution

Collecting taxes is also a federal duty. All working people in the United States must pay federal taxes. This money helps keep the country running. The federal level also decides how to **dole** out tax dollars.

The federal level deals in other money matters. It sets the national currency. This is the cash found in people's wallets. The redesign of bills and coins is up to people at this level as well.

Agencies are also run at the federal level. These are departments that take care of certain tasks. A well-known agency is the Food and Drug Administration (FDA). The FDA plays a key role. It is in charge of food safety. It also ensures that medicines are safe for use. Their core task is to protect U.S. public health.

Equity for All

For many people, social justice is an important issue facing the country. The federal government can help set the course for social justice in the United States. In 2021, President Joe Biden signed several executive orders on his first day in office. One order required that "the Federal Government should pursue a comprehensive approach to advancing equity for all."

State Significance

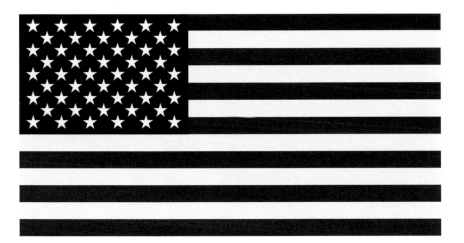

The U.S. flag has 50 stars. Each star represents a state. That means that there are 50 state governments. Two other state-level governments also exist. These are found in Puerto Rico and Washington, DC.

States' powers come from the U.S. Constitution. The Tenth Amendment defines the U.S. federal government. It outlines federal powers. All other powers fall to the states and the people.

Each state is distinct. People who live in Oregon, for example, face certain issues. They have their own expectations of their state government. But in Florida, citizens may face different issues. They might want other matters addressed. Each state acts and responds in its own way.

State governments have a lot of power. This level of government takes care of a long list of issues. States can make big decisions for their people.

Testing for Democracy

Some people call state government a "laboratory for democracy." There are diverse views in each U.S. state. New policy ideas emerge in each one. For instance, a state might decide to raise the minimum wage for workers. Other states might watch this new policy to see how it turns out. Later, the wage increase might even be adopted at the national level.

Is It a State?

Washington DC, Puerto Rico, and several other U.S. territories are not states. This can be a **contentious** issue. People who live in these places are taxpayers, and most are U.S. citizens. But they do not have state status. They do not have the same representation in Congress that people in states have. This means that their issues are not always addressed by the government.

House of Representatives
chamber, Idaho State Capitol

State Duties

Most people in the United States mainly interact with their state or local governments. The states deal with issues that most concern their people.

For starters, the states hand out many important official documents. Each document provides proof that something happened. When someone is born, they receive a birth certificate. This paper has great value. It sets up someone's citizenship rights. It is needed to get a passport or meet other personal identification requirements.

Death certificates are ordered at the end of a life. Marriage certificates prove a union between two people. All these papers are crucial. And each one is up to the state level to provide.

The state government is also important for people who want to drive. Every state has a Department of Motor Vehicles. Anyone in need of a driver's license goes through this department. Vehicle registration is covered here. States set speed limits for roads, too.

States **license** many professional workers. Doctors, teachers, lawyers, and more all need a license to do their work in that state. The state handles their licensing exams. Once licensed, they can begin to work in that state.

Alabama State Capitol

Constitution Care

Constitutions are not limited to the federal level. Every state also has its own constitution. Each one outlines the rights and freedoms of the state's people. It also covers the state's duties. Alabama has the longest U.S. state constitution with more than 376,000 words!

CONSTITUTION OF TENNESSEE.

I.

TENNESSEE'S CONSTITUTIONS.

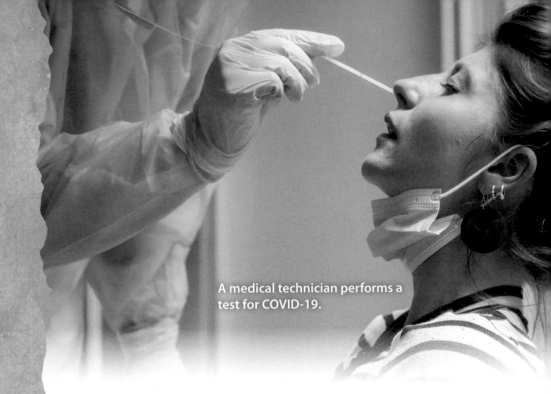

A medical technician performs a test for COVID-19.

Pandemic Response

March 2020 marked a grim beginning. COVID-19 was a disease spreading across the world. It passed easily from person to person. The World Health Organization declared a global pandemic. Major shutdowns followed. No country was immune to the spread.

This was a global public health issue. In America, states are in charge of public health. Each state is tasked with the safety of its residents. During this crisis, the care of people was largely up to the states.

Each state responded in its own way. The leaders had unique approaches. Schools shut down and reopened at different times. Testing measures varied. States even went into **lockdowns**. But each differed in the details.

The pandemic affected vulnerable groups of people the most. Older people were most in danger. People of color also faced a greater impact. Some states responded to this racial **disparity**.

For many people, public health became a top priority. People in the United States had a range of concerns during the pandemic. It was up to the states to handle many of them. State governments led the way during a very uncertain time.

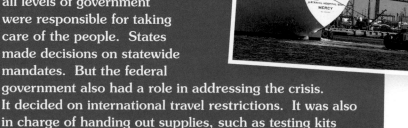

All Hands on Deck

Throughout the pandemic, all levels of government were responsible for taking care of the people. States made decisions on statewide mandates. But the federal government also had a role in addressing the crisis. It decided on international travel restrictions. It was also in charge of handing out supplies, such as testing kits and masks.

Local Leadership

There is one federal government in America. State governments also have powers. But there is a much higher tally of local governments. There are over 90,000 in total!

The local level is often the most vital level for people in the United States. The president gets a lot of screen time. National leadership is crucial. But for most people, local leadership will have a greater impact on their lives.

Former Shreveport Mayor Ollie Tyler (center) leads a meeting in Louisiana.

CITY HALL

Fluctuating Data

The number of local governments has gone up and down over the years. In 1942, there were 155,116 local governments across America. Now, that number has dipped to under 100,000. Why the change? Special districts are created and **dissolved** every year.

Five Types

There are five types of local governments. First, there are counties. Second, there are **municipalities**. Third, there are townships. Lastly, there are special districts and school districts.

The first three types of government stay constant. Each one is the main government in a region. Sometimes, they serve a defined part of the population. Others provide services to an outlined area. These governments have a wide range of duties.

School and special districts have more specific tasks. Each has a main purpose. The number of districts changes every year. A special district may fix street lighting in an area. Or, it might be in charge of the region's water supply.

counties

municipalities

townships

special districts

school districts

County vs. Municipality

Counties serve large areas. Each one does not serve just one city or town. This type of government exists within a state. Each county is, of course, never as large as its state. Counties also go by different names. In Alaska, they are known as *boroughs*. In Louisiana, they are known as *parishes*.

Municipalities often serve a city, town, or community. Each one tends to center around a large number of people. The size differences among municipalities can be great. Millions of people live in New York City. This city is one municipality. Los Angeles is another. It, too, is home to millions of people. But municipalities can be much smaller as well. One might only serve a few hundred people.

County Commitments

Like all governments, the local level is there to serve its people. It deals with many vital issues.

Counties provide a number of services. A U.S. county often has one or more courthouses. Each one employs a number of county officials. A county clerk is one of them. County clerks are tasked with voter registration.

local government building, Maine

Counties also help maintain public services. These can range from hospitals to airports to public transportation.

State to Local

Remember the separation of powers between federal and state governments? Both levels share powers and responsibilities according to the U.S. Constitution. In contrast, local governments must be granted power by the state.

Missouri State Capitol

Municipal Missions

Municipalities also serve their people. These governments have some overlap with counties. The municipal level helps with public transportation. Leaders at this level review bus routes. Adding new subway lines is also their decision to make.

If a person needs emergency help, they will likely dial 911. This is a connection to first responders. A person in distress can then get the help they need. Firefighters may be sent. Ambulances are called to transport someone in medical need. Municipalities help maintain these services.

sanitation worker

Garbage collection is also a local duty. Some citizens might wonder about recycling options. Others may want to see more composting choices. The local level addresses all these needs.

Get in Touch

Americans all have civic duties. One duty is to speak up about community concerns. The U.S. government's website has options to contact the president or other White House staff. But contacting a local government official is often a more effective way to be heard.

Fun in a community is often found in its public spaces. For many people, a great day is one spent at a local park. For others, joy is found playing on a sports field. For bookworms, libraries open up a world of knowledge. These are all public spaces. Everyone has **access** to them. Municipalities are charged with taking care of these community areas.

Another concern for the local level is street maintenance. It is up to municipalities to fix potholes. If there is snow, the local government helps clear the public roads.

subway, Queens, New York

Working Together

Each level of government has its own task list. Certain duties are theirs only. But the different levels sometimes work together to solve issues. This teamwork is crucial for smooth operations.

Some government powers are exclusive. But **concurrent** powers are shared. More than one level of government has control. This means it is up to both levels to solve certain issues.

Duo Duties

Every young person in America has the right to free public education. This is a hefty responsibility. Both local and state governments share this duty.

Educational standards are up to state leaders. What are the learning goals of each grade? What subjects should be taught? How can the curriculum be structured? These questions are answered at a state level. The local level deals with the nuts-and-bolts of running schools. This level hires teachers. Building schools is also their responsibility.

Yosemite National Park, California

The federal and state levels both take care of natural spaces. America is known for its vast landscapes. Forests and grasslands define the country. It is home to both state and national parks. Both levels protect these natural areas. The federal level runs the National Park System (NPS). Every state is home to an area in the NPS.

Voting Values

The federal and local governments team up for another large issue: voting. The federal level, through the U.S. Constitution, decides the standards for running national elections. Local governments, under the watchful eye of states, set up polling stations and keep voter registers.

Trio Tasks

In America, there are over 4 million miles (6.4 million kilometers) of roads. That is a lot of pavement to keep up! Local governments are in charge of local roads. But there are many stretches of U.S. highways. Keeping these roads smooth is a task for all government levels. Nearly 97 percent of roads are up to the local and state levels to maintain. The federal level looks after roads running through national parks.

Public safety is also a concern for all levels. Each level of government directs people in law enforcement. The federal level steers the group looking after national matters. This is the Federal Bureau of Investigation (FBI). Preventing terrorism is one of its tasks. State troopers work throughout a state. Most often, they patrol highways and roads. Most cities or towns also have local police. These agencies are more specific to an area. Duties range for each level.

New Hampshire highway

Finally, part of living and working in the United States is paying taxes. There are taxes that fund each level of government. Most income tax goes to the federal level. Income tax is a percentage of a worker's paycheck. Sales taxes mainly fund the states. These are taxes on items or services that are bought. Property taxes go to local governments. People pay these taxes for the land on which their businesses or homes sit.

Federal Tax   State Tax

Paycheck

0000

DATE _____ 20 _____

PAY TO THE
ORDER OF _____ $ _____

_____ DOLLARS 🔒 SECURITY FEATURES ARE INCLUDED DETAILS ON BACK

MEMO _____ _____

⑆ 0⑈234356789 ⑉   0⑈234356789⑉   ⑈234

This diagram shows the approximate percentage of a worker's pay that goes to different taxes.

Sales Tax ↑

Value Your Vote

Voting is one way U.S. citizens can create change and stand up for issues that matter to them. If you are an American, you must be 18 years old to vote. But in some states, you can pre-register to vote when you are as young as 16. Find out how you can register to vote so you are ready for your first election!

Civic Commitments

How can we make a difference in our communities? This question is important for many people in the United States. Every person has their own civic concerns. But sometimes, it is hard to know how to address these concerns. It is also tricky to know which leaders to turn to for help.

A government is built to serve its people. The three levels all deal with specific issues. Learning about your community is key. Understanding how government works is how you know who to ask for help with issues.

Identify the issues that matter to you. What concerns do you have for the future of your community? Addressing climate concerns can be an immense task. The future of education might also interest you. Social justice may be an issue close to your heart. Or the state of the economy might be your concern. These are just some of the issues that government deals with.

People gather to support a cause.

Meaningful change takes time. But we can help set it in motion by speaking up. Connecting with local leadership can be a first step. Participating in a rally might be another path. In your future, running for government office can be a great thing to do as well.

Spend some time reflecting now. Different levels of government help solve issues. But people can also make a difference. How will you help solve issues in your community?

Stay Curious

The global community is facing a lot of tough issues. Sometimes, these concerns can seem overwhelming. But it helps to focus on what we can control—our actions. Staying curious and speaking up on issues that matter is one way forward. Together, we can find creative solutions to our biggest national and global issues.

Map It!

Map out the local governments in your area. Ask a friend or two to join you in creating a map.

1. Find a large piece of paper and pens or markers.
2. If you live in the United States, sketch the outline of your state. If you live outside the United States, choose a state your group is curious about. Draw an outline of this state on your paper.
3. Every state is home to many local governments. Begin researching what counties or municipalities are in the state of your choosing. A great place to start your research is **www.usa.gov/local-governments**.
4. On your state map, sketch the areas for three local governments. Label each area with the name of the county or municipality.
5. Look up each county's or municipality's population. How many people are served by each of the three local governments? Write these numbers next to each area.
6. Notice the different shapes of the three counties and municipalities. Do you see any similarities? Do you spy any differences?
7. **Bonus:** Who is the leader of each local government? Write their name beside each section on the map.

LaSalle
county

Illinois

McDonough
county

Cumberland
county

Glossary

access—a way of being able to use or get something

amend—to change

concurrent—happening or used at the same time

contentious—likely to cause arguments or disagreements

disparity—a large and often unfair difference between people or things

disputes—disagreements

dissolved—officially ended

diverse—made up of people or things that are different from each other

dole—to give something to people

federalism—a system of government in which the same area is controlled by at least two levels of government

governance—the way that a city or place is controlled and run by the people in leadership roles

interact—to talk or do things with other people or systems

license—to give an individual the right to do a job, such as work as a lawyer, doctor, or public-school teacher

lockdowns—short-term conditions imposed by government in which people must stay in their homes and limit their activities outside the home where they come into contact with others

municipalities—towns or cities that have their own local governments

pandemic—a widespread outbreak of disease that quickly affects a lot of people across a wide area

unified—being all in agreement

New Mexico State Capitol

Index

Learn More!

It can be good to get to know your leaders. If you live in the United States, look up your local leader or a community leader. Then, find out who your state governor is. Finally, start looking for details about the current U.S. president.

If you live outside the United States, first choose a state. Then, look up the mayor of the state's capital city. Find out the state's governor next. Finally, find some data on the current U.S. president.

✻ Create a poster with profile details about each leader, as well as which level of government they govern.

✻ List some of the major decisions each leader has made while in office.

✻ What differences do you notice?

✻ Look for newspaper articles with quotations from them. What have they said that catches your eye?

✻ Share your findings with your classmates.

Ohio State Capitol